Learn to Read
Russian in 5 Days

SERGEI ORLOV

ISBN-13: 978-1-988800-01-1

CONTENTS

Introduction   i

Unit 1 – а, о, к, м, т   1

Unit 2 – у, р, с, в   3

Unit 3 – и, н, х, б   5

Unit 4 – л, п, д, е   7

Unit 5 – ы, г, з, ч   9

Unit 6 – й, ц, ш, ж   11

Unit 7 – я, ю, ё   13

Unit 8 – ф, э, щ   15

Unit 9 – ь, ъ   17

Unit 10 – Review   19

Russian Alphabet   21

Glossary – Thematic Order   23

Glossary – Alphabetical Order   31

INTRODUCTION

Learning a new alphabet can be very intimidating for an English speaker only used to reading the Latin alphabet. This is partly why English speakers tend to stick to learning other languages that use the same alphabet, such as French, Spanish and Italian – because they seem a lot easier!

But learning a new alphabet does not have to be so difficult. The difficulty is finding a good system to learn the new alphabet so that you don't get discouraged and give up before you make real progress.

The secret to learning a new alphabet is to be taught how to pronounce each letter separately, and then to practice how the new letters combine with letters you already know to read real words in the alphabet in a structured way. This is not revolutionary – it is probably how you learned to read English – but it is not easy to find for other languages.

This book will teach you how to read the Russian alphabet in exactly that way, and with this method you will be able to read Russian in only 5 days or less! After that you will be able to enjoy the Russian language and culture in a way that you were never able to before.

THE RUSSIAN ALPHABET
русский алфавит

The Russian language uses 33 letters of the Cyrillic alphabet and is written from left to right. It uses the same basic alphabet as several other Slavic languages, including Ukrainian and Bulgarian, although there are differences in pronunciation between Russian and other languages that use the Cyrillic alphabet, just like there are differences in pronunciation between French, Spanish and English even though they use the same alphabet.

Although it does not closely resemble the Latin alphabet used to write English (and other European languages) it is not a difficult alphabet to learn to read. This is because, for the most part, letters are pronounced as they are written and written as they are pronounced, unlike languages such as English that make use of a lot of silent letters and historical spellings. Although correct Russian pronunciation can be difficult for English speakers, learning to read the alphabet is not as much as a challenge as it at first seems.

Like the Latin alphabet used to write English, the Russian alphabet has both upper and lower case letters. Upper case letters are used at the beginning of a sentence and in proper nouns.

HOW TO USE THIS COURSE

The primary goal of this course book is to teach the reader to recognize the Russian alphabet and to begin to read the Russian language.

The main way this is accomplished is by teaching the individual pronunciations of each letter, and then utilizing "Practice" sections where the student can practice reading real Russian words. These "Practice" sections are very important and the main way the student will start to feel comfortable with the Russian alphabet. The answers to all "Practice" questions are included directly below the questions, but try to avoid looking at the answers until you have attempted to answer the questions yourself.

Throughout the book, the reader will also learn approximately 150 real Russian words. These words have been carefully selected to be of maximum benefit to beginner students of the language and are a great starting point for students who want to continue their study of Russian. In the end of the book there are two glossaries – one in thematic order and one in alphabetical order – where the student can study and memorize all the words learned in this course.
The course material has been designed to be completed slowly over

5 days, while reviewing lessons as necessary. You are encouraged to go at whatever pace you feel comfortable with and to feel free to go back to lessons to review as much as needed.

Good luck and I hope you enjoy the first step on your journey to learning the Russian language.

UNIT 1 - а, о, к, м, т

The first 5 letters introduced in this course are the letters in Russian that resemble English letters and are pronounced roughly the same. Basically you already know these five Russian letters!

The letter а in Russian is pronounced like the "a" sound in the English words "spa" or "father" (IPA: /a/). The uppercase form is А.

The letter о is pronounced like the "o" sound in the English word "hope" (IPA: /o/) when stressed. When this letter is not stressed in a word, it is pronounced like the "o" in "harmony" which makes it basically the same as a Russian "a". The uppercase form is О.

The letter к is pronounced like the "k" sound in the English words "kick" or "kite" (IPA: /k/). The uppercase form is К.

The letter м is pronounced like the "m" sound in the English words "mother" or "Michael" (IPA: /m/). The uppercase form is М.

The letter т is pronounced like the "t" sound in the English words "tan" or "Tom" (IPA: /t/). The uppercase form is Т.

As you can see these 5 letters are virtually the same as in English!

PRACTICE

Try to recognize these English words in their Russian disguises. The answers are below.

1. ат
2. кат
3. так
4. кот
5. мат
6. мама

ANSWERS

1. at
2. cat
3. tack
4. coat
5. mat
6. mama

UNIT 2 - y, p, c, в

The four letters introduced in this unit look like English letters, but unlike Unit 1 these letters are not pronounced the same as in English. Pay close attention to these letters when reading Russian, as their similarity to letters in English make them an easy source of confusion.

The letter y is pronounced like the "oo" sound in "boot", or the end of the word "shoe". (IPA: /u/). It is not pronounced like the "y" sound in the English words "yellow" or "tiny". The pronunciation will be represented by "u" in this book. The uppercase form is У.

The letter p is pronounced like the Spanish "r" sound in "rapido", i.e. a trilled or rolled "r" sound (IPA: /r/). This letter is not difficult to pronounce for an English speaker but does require some practice. If you cannot pronounce this letter yet, you can substitute an English "r" sound for now. Although this letter resembles an English "p" it is not pronounced like a "p" sound. The uppercase form is P.

The letter c is pronounced like the "s" sound in "some" or "same" (IPA: /s/). Although it resembles an English "c", it is never pronounced like the "c" in "cat". It is always pronounced with an "s" sound. The hard "c" sound is spelled with к in Russian. The uppercase form is C.

The letter в is pronounced like the "v" sound in "very" (IPA: /v/). Although this letter resembles an uppercase "B", it is never pronounced like the English "b" sound in "boy". The uppercase form is B.

PRACTICE

Try to recognize these English words in their Russian disguises. Focus on the correct pronunciation and not necessarily the English spelling. The answers are below.

1. рат
2. сат
3. рум
4. катс
5. мотор
6. мут
7. тум
8. васт
9. стов
10. сторм

ANSWERS

1. rat
2. sat
3. room
4. cats
5. motor
6. moot
7. tomb
8. vast
9. stove
10. storm

UNIT 3 - и, н, х, б

The Russian letter и, which looks like an uppercase "N" written backwards, is pronounced like the "ee" sound in "bee" or the "i" sound in "spaghetti" (IPA: /i/). The pronunciation will be represented by "i" in this book. The uppercase form is И.

The Russian letter н is pronounced like the "n" sound in "now" or "hen" (IPA: /n/). Pay close attention to this letter as it resembles an uppercase "H" in English, but should not be pronounced with an "h" sound. The uppercase form is H.

The pronunciation of the Russian letter х does not exist in English. It is the "ch" sound in the German "doch" or the "j" sound in the Spanish "ojos". It is a heavy throat clearing "h" sound (IPA: /x/). The pronunciation will be represented by "kh" in this book. The uppercase form is X.

The letter б is pronounced like the "b" sound in "best" (IPA: /b/). Pay close attention to the letters б and в. The letter б, which looks like the number "6" is pronounced "b" and the letter в, which looks like an uppercase "B", is pronounced "v". With some practice this will become easier. The uppercase form is Б.

THE ACCENT IN RUSSIAN

Like English, in Russian to pronounce a word correctly one must stress one syllable over the others. Also like English, the accent in Russian is not normally written. Think about the English word conduct. It can be pronounced CONduct, or conDUCT although the written language does not tell us which one is correct. This is the same as the situation in Russian.

In Russian-English dictionaries you will often see an accent written on the vowel that is to be stressed in the Russian word. These accents, however, are not normally written in the language and therefore I will not be including them in the Russian words in this book. However, I have included the accent in the pronunciation so that readers can learn to pronounce the words correctly.

PRACTICE

Try to read these real Russian words. The English translation is given next to each word. The correct pronunciations (with accents) are given in the answers below.

1. вино   (wine)
2. ухо   (ear)
3. три   (three)
4. нос   (nose)
5. банк   (bank)
6. брат   (brother)

ANSWERS

1. vinó
2. úkho
3. tri
4. nos
5. bank
6. brat

UNIT 4 - л, п, д, е

The Russian letter л is pronounced like the "l" sound in "little" or "like" (IPA: /l/). The uppercase form is Л.

The letter п is pronounced like the "p" sound in "pie" or "pepper" (IPA: /p/). The Russian letter resembles the Greek letter pi that you probably remember from geometry. This is not a coincidence as the Cyrillic alphabet derives from the Greek alphabet and some letters are very similar. The uppercase form is П.

The letter д is pronounced like the "d" sound in "dad" (IPA: /d/). The uppercase form is Д.

The letter е is pronounced like the "ye" sound in "yes" (IPA: /je/). When е is preceded by a consonant, it causes the consonant to "soften". This softening (technically called palatalization) is a light "y" sound pronounced at the end of the consonant sound.

Compare the English words "moot" and "mute". The light "y" sound in "mute" is that softening. After a consonant this softening will be represented by a ' (apostrophe) before the "e" in the pronunciations. Remember that this ' means there is a slight "y" sound. The uppercase form of е is Е.

PRACTICE

Try to read these Russian words. The English translation is given next to each word. The correct pronunciations are given in the answers below.

1. да   (yes)
2. нет   (no)
3. лодка   (boat)
4. стул   (chair)
5. тело   (body)
6. дом   (house)
7. хлеб   (bread)
8. пиво   (beer)
9. еда   (food)
10. велосипед   (bicycle)

ANSWERS

1. da
2. n'et
3. lódka
4. stul
5. t'élo
6. dom
7. khl'eb
8. pívo
9. yedá
10. v'elosip'éd

UNIT 5 - ы, г, з, ч

The Russian letter ы, which looks like a small "bl", is pronounced close to the "i" sound in "rid" (IPA: /ɨ/). Note that this is not the same sound as the Russian letter и. To distinguish these two letters, ы will be represented in this book as "y" as this is standard practice when writing Russian words in English. Remember however that this is a short "i" sound and not a "y" sound or an "ee" sound. The uppercase form is Ы.

The letter г is pronounced like the "g" sound in "good" (IPA: /g/). The uppercase form is Г.

The letter з is pronounced like the "z" sound in "zoo" (IPA: /z/). This letter resembles the number "3". The uppercase form is З.

The letter ч is pronounced like the "ch" sound in "church" (IPA: /tʃ/). Although written with two letters in English, it is really a single sound and is only written with one letter in Russian. This letter will be represented in the pronunciations by č. The uppercase form is Ч.

PRACTICE

Try to read these Russian words. The English translation is given next to each word. The correct pronunciations are given in the answers below.

1. сыр   (cheese)
2. сын   (son)
3. рыба   (fish)

4. друг   (friend)
5. город   (city)
6. глаз   (eye)
7. магазин   (store / shop)
8. озеро   (lake)
9. час   (hour)
10. человек   (person)

ANSWERS

1. syr
2. syn
3. rýba
4. drug
5. górod
6. glaz
7. magazín
8. óz'ero
9. čas
10. č'elov'ék

UNIT 6 - й, ц, ш, ж

The letter й is pronounced like the "y" sound in "toy", i.e. it creates a diphthong out of the preceding vowel (IPA: /j/). The letter й consists of the letter и with a *breve* above it. It is a separate letter in Russian, however. It will be represented in the pronunciation as either a "i" or a "y" after another vowel to attempt to represent the pronunciation correctly in English. The uppercase form is Й.

The letter ц is pronounced like the "ts" sound in "cats" (IPA: /ts/). This is really two sounds, a "t" sound followed by an "s" sound, but it is written with only one letter in Russian. When writing Russian words in English this letter is often represented by a "c", but in this book I will use "ts" to avoid confusion with the English "c" sound. Unlike English, in Russian this letter can be used at the beginning of a word and is still pronounced "ts". The uppercase form is Ц.

The letter ш is pronounced like the "sh" sound in "short" (IPA: /ʃ/). Although written with two letters in English, it is really one sound and it is written with one letter in Russian. This letter will be represented in this book by š. The uppercase form is Ш.

The letter ж is pronounced like the "s" sound in "pleasure" or "measure" (IPA: /ʒ/). This letter will be represented in this book as ž. The uppercase form is Ж.

PRACTICE

Try to read these Russian words. The English translation is given next to each word. The correct pronunciations are given in the answers below.

1. чай   (tea)
2. плохой   (bad)
3. синий   (blue)
4. лицо   (face)
5. улица   (street)
6. цвет   (color)
7. рубашка   (shirt)
8. школа   (school)
9. ужин   (dinner)
10. одежда   (clothing)

ANSWERS

1. čai
2. ploxóy
3. síniy
4. litsó
5. úlitsa
6. tsv'et
7. rubáška
8. škóla
9. úžin
10. od'éžda

UNIT 7 - я, ю, ё

The three letters introduced in this unit all begin with a "y" sound followed by a vowel sound, and cause the preceding consonant to "soften" like е.

The letter я is pronounced like the "ya" sound in "yard" (IPA: /ja/). Like е, this letter will be represented in the pronunciation by "ya" at the beginning of a word or after a vowel, and as 'a after a consonant to represent the consonant's "softening". This letter looks like a backwards capital "R". The uppercase form is Я.

The letter ю is pronounced like "you", i.e. a "y" sound followed by a "u" (IPA: /ju/). ю follows the same pronunciation rules as е and я. The uppercase form is Ю

The letter ё is pronounced like the "yo" sound in "yoghurt" (IPA: /jo/) and follows the same softening rules as the other letters in this unit. This letter always receives the stress in a Russian word. Often this letter is written without the dots above the letter, which makes it look the same as е. The uppercase form is Ё.

Remember that the ' (apostrophe) in the pronunciation indicates there should be a slight "y" sound before the vowel.

PRACTICE

Try to read these Russian words. The English translation is given next to each word. The correct pronunciations are given in the answers below.

1. шляпа   (hat)
2. мясо   (meat)
3. яблоко   (apple)
4. брюки   (pants)
5. лёд   (ice)
6. чёрный   (black)

ANSWERS

1. šl'ápa
2. m'áso
3. yábloko
4. br'úki
5. l'od
6. č'órnyy

UNIT 8 - ф, э, щ

The three letters in this unit are relatively rare in Russian compared to the previous letters.

The letter ф is pronounced like the "f" sound in "far" (IPA: /f/). The uppercase form is Ф.

The letter э is pronounced like the "e" in "economics" (IPA: /ɛ/). It is used at the beginning of a word or after a vowel instead of е when the pronunciation should be "e" and not "ye". The uppercase form is Э.

The letter щ is pronounced with a "soft" s sound (IPA: /ɕ/). It is like the š sound but softer and pronounced more towards the front of your mouth - like a "sy". Beginners can pronounce this letter with a "sh" sound in the beginning, but should practice the correct pronunciation with a native speaker when possible. This letter is often written "shch" when Russian words or names are written in English, however it is no longer pronounced with a "sh" and a "ch". This letter will be written š' in the pronunciation in this book. The uppercase form is Щ.

PRACTICE

Try to read these Russian words that have been borrowed from English. Try to guess the pronunciation and the English word. The answers are below.

1. кофе   (coffee)
2. туфля   (shoe)
3. аэропорт   (airport)
4. женщина   (woman)

ANSWERS

1. kófʼe
2. túflya
3. aeropórt
4. žʼénšʼina

UNIT 9 - ь, ъ

The letter **ь** is called a soft sign. The soft sign is normally written after a consonant and indicates its "softening". We have already looked at softening with the vowels that have a "y" pronunciation, **е, ё, я** and **ю**. These four vowels automatically cause the preceding consonant to soften. When a consonant needs to soften without one of these four vowels, the soft sign **ь** is used. This softening will be represented by ' (apostrophe) in the pronunciation.

The letter **ъ** is called a hard sign. Its use is the exact opposite of **ь**, i.e. it takes a "soft" consonant and makes it "hard" again. This letter is however extremely rare in Modern Russian and can be ignored for now. There are no words in this book that use this letter. If you do ever see it just pronounce the consonant normally and otherwise ignore the letter **ъ**.

PRACTICE

Try to read these Russian words. Pay attention to the **ь**. The English translation is given next to each word. The correct pronunciations are given in the answers below.

1. мышь   (mouse)
2. мать   (mother)
3. дочь   (daughter)
4. лошадь   (horse)
5. дверь   (door)

ANSWERS

1. myš'
2. mat'
3. doč'
4. lóšad'
5. dv'er'

UNIT 10 - REVIEW

PRACTICE 1

Review the previous lessons by reading these real Russian place names below. The correct pronunciations are given in the answers below.

1. Россия
2. Москва
3. Санкт-Петербург
4. Нижний Новгород
5. Сибирь
6. Волга
7. Чёрное море
8. Каспийское море
9. Озеро Байкал
10. Уральские горы

ANSWERS 1

1. Rossíya (Russia)
2. Moskvá
3. Sankt-P'et'erbúrg
4. Nižnyy Nóvgorod
5. Sibír' (Siberia)
6. Vólga
7. Č'ornoye mór'e (Black Sea)
8. Kaspíyskoye mór'e (Caspian Sea)
9. Óz'ero Baikál (Lake Baikal)
10. Urál'skiye Góry (Ural Mountains)

PRACTICE 2

Review what you have learned in this book by reading the Russian names below. The correct pronunciations are given in the answers below.

1. Путин
2. Медведев
3. Ельцин
4. Горбачёв
5. Хрущёв
6. Толстой
7. Достоевский
8. Гагарин

ANSWERS 2

1. Pútin
2. Medv'éd'ev
3. Yél'tsin
4. Gorbač'ov (Gorbachev)
5. Khrúš'ov (Khrushchev)
6. Tolstóy
7. Dostoyévskiy
8. Gagárin

RUSSIAN ALPHABET

Uppercase	Lowercase	Pronunciation
А	а	[a]
Б	б	[b]
В	в	[v]
Г	г	[g]
Д	д	[d]
Е	е	[ye]
Ё	ё	[yo]
Ж	ж	[ž]
З	з	[z]
И	и	[i]
Й	й	[y]
К	к	[k]
Л	л	[l]
М	м	[m]
Н	н	[n]

О	о	[o]
П	п	[p]
Р	р	[r]
С	с	[s]
Т	т	[t]
У	у	[u]
Ф	ф	[f]
Х	х	[kh]
Ц	ц	[ts]
Ч	ч	[č]
Ш	ш	[š]
Щ	щ	[š']
Ъ	ъ	
Ы	ы	[y]
Ь	ь	[']
Э	э	[e]
Ю	ю	[yu]
Я	я	[ya]

GLOSSARY – THEMATIC ORDER

ANIMALS

животное	[živótnoye]	animal
собака	[sobáka]	dog
кошка	[kóška]	cat
рыба	[rýba]	fish
птица	[ptítsa]	bird
корова	[koróva]	cow
свинья	[svin'yá]	pig
мышь	[myš']	mouse
лошадь	[lóšad']	horse

PEOPLE

человек	[č'elov'ék]	person
мать	[mat']	mother
мама	[máma]	mommy / mama
отец	[ot'éts]	father
папа	[pápa]	daddy / papa
сын	[syn]	son
дочь	[doč']	daughter
брат	[brat]	brother
сестра	[s'estrá]	sister
друг	[drug]	friend
мужчина	[mužčína]	man
женщина	[ž'énš'ina]	woman
мальчик	[mál'čik]	boy
девушка	[d'évuška]	girl
ребёнок	[reb'ónok]	child

TRANSPORTATION

поезд	[póyezd]	train
самолёт	[samol'ót]	airplane
машина	[mašína]	car (automobile)
велосипед	[v'elosip'éd]	bicycle
автобус	[avtóbus]	bus
лодка	[lódka]	boat

LOCATION

город	[górod]	city
дом	[dom]	house
улица	[úlitsa]	street
аэропорт	[aeropórt]	airport
гостиница	[gostínitsa]	hotel
ресторан	[restorán]	restaurant
школа	[škóla]	school
университет	[univ'ersit'ét]	university
парк	[park]	park
магазин	[magazín]	store / shop
больница	[bol'nítsa]	hospital
церковь	[ts'érkov']	church
страна	[straná]	country (state)
банк	[bank]	bank
рынок	[rýnok]	market

HOME

стол	[stol]	table
стул	[stul]	chair
окно	[oknó]	window
дверь	[dv'er']	door
книга	[kníga]	book

CLOTHING

одежда	[od'éžda]	clothing
шляпа	[šl'ápa]	hat
платье	[plát'ye]	dress
рубашка	[rubáška]	shirt
брюки	[br'úki]	pants
туфля	[túflya]	shoe

BODY

тело	[t'élo]	body
голова	[golová]	head
лицо	[litsó]	face
волосы	[vólosy]	hair
глаз	[glaz]	eye
рот	[rot]	mouth
нос	[nos]	nose
ухо	[úkho]	ear
рука	[ruká]	hand / arm
нога	[nogá]	foot / leg
сердце	[s'érdts'e]	heart
кровь	[krov']	blood

кость	[kost']	bone
борода	[borodá]	beard

MISCELLANEOUS

да	[da]	yes
нет	[n'et]	no

FOOD & DRINK

еда	[yedá]	food
мясо	[m'áso]	meat
хлеб	[khl'eb]	bread
сыр	[syr]	cheese
яблоко	[yábloko]	apple
вода	[vodá]	water
пиво	[pívo]	beer
вино	[vinó]	wine
кофе	[kóf'e]	coffee
чай	[čái]	tea
молоко	[molokó]	milk
завтрак	[závtrak]	breakfast
обед	[ob'éd]	lunch
ужин	[úžin]	dinner

COLORS

цвет	[tsv'et]	color
красный	[krásnyy]	red
синий	[síniy]	blue
зелёный	[z'el'ónyy]	green

жёлтый	[ž'óltyy]	yellow
чёрный	[č'órnyy]	black
белый	[b'élyy]	white

NATURE

море	[mór'e]	sea
река	[r'eká]	river
озеро	[óz'ero]	lake
гора	[gorá]	mountain
дождь	[dožd']	rain
снег	[sn'eg]	snow
дерево	[d'ér'evo]	tree
цветок	[tsv'etók]	flower
солнце	[sólnts'e]	sun
луна	[luná]	moon
ветер	[v'ét'er]	wind
небо	[n'ébo]	sky
огонь	[ogón']	fire
лёд	[l'od]	ice

ADJECTIVES

большой	[bol'šóy]	big
маленький	[mál'en'kiy]	small
хороший	[khoróšiy]	good
плохой	[ploxóy]	bad
горячий	[gor'áčiy]	hot
холодный	[kholódnyy]	cold
дешёвый	[d'eš'óvyy]	cheap
дорогой	[dorogóy]	expensive

| счастливый | [sčastlívyy] | happy |
| грустный | [grústnyy] | sad |

NUMBERS

один	[odín]	one
два	[dva]	two
три	[tri]	three
четыре	[četýr'e]	four
пять	[pyat']	five
шесть	[š'est']	six
семь	[s'em']	seven
восемь	[vós'em']	eight
девять	[d'ev'at']	nine
десять	[d'es'at']	ten

TIME

день	[d'en']	day
месяц	[m'ésyats]	month
год	[god]	year
час	[čas]	hour
сегодня	[s'evódnya]	today
завтра	[závtra]	tomorrow
вчера	[vč'erá]	yesterday

DAYS OF THE WEEK

воскресенье	[voskr'esén'ye]	Sunday
понедельник	[pon'edél'nik]	Monday
вторник	[vtórnik]	Tuesday
среда	[sr'edá]	Wednesday
четверг	[č'etv'érg]	Thursday
пятница	[pyátnitsa]	Friday
суббота	[subbóta]	Saturday

MONTHS

январь	[yanvár']	January
февраль	[f'evrál']	February
март	[mart]	March
апрель	[apr'él']	April
май	[mai]	May
июнь	[iyún']	June
июль	[iyúl']	July
август	[ávgust]	August
сентябрь	[s'entyábr']	September
октябрь	[oktyábr']	October
ноябрь	[noyábr']	November
декабрь	[d'ekábr']	December

PROPER NAMES

Россия	[rosíya]	Russia
русский	[rúskiy]	Russian
Москва	[moskvá]	Moscow

GLOSSARY – ALPHABETICAL ORDER

– A a –

август	[ávgust]	August
автобус	[avtóbus]	bus
апрель	[apr'él']	April
аэропорт	[aeropórt]	airport

– Б б –

банк	[bank]	bank
белый	[b'élyy]	white
больница	[bol'nítsa]	hospital
большой	[bol'šóy]	big
борода	[borodá]	beard
брат	[brat]	brother
брюки	[br'úki]	pants

– В в –

велосипед	[v'elosip'éd]	bicycle
ветер	[v'ét'er]	wind
вино	[vinó]	wine
вода	[vodá]	water
волосы	[vólosy]	hair
восемь	[vós'em']	eight
воскресенье	[voskr'esén'ye]	Sunday
вторник	[vtórnik]	Tuesday
вчера	[vč'erá]	yesterday

– Г г –

глаз	[glaz]	eye
год	[god]	year
голова	[golová]	head
гора	[gorá]	mountain
город	[górod]	city
горячий	[gor'áčiy]	hot
гостиница	[gostínitsa]	hotel
грустный	[grústnyy]	sad

– Д д –

да	[da]	yes
два	[dva]	two
дверь	[dv'er']	door
девушка	[d'évuška]	girl
девять	[d'ev'at']	nine
декабрь	[d'ekábr']	December
день	[d'en']	day
дерево	[d'ér'evo]	tree
десять	[d'es'at']	ten
дешёвый	[d'eš'óvyy]	cheap
дождь	[dožd']	rain
дом	[dom]	house
дорогой	[dorogóy]	expensive
дочь	[doč']	daughter
друг	[drug]	friend

– Е е –

| еда | [yedá] | food |

32

– Ж ж –

жёлтый	[ž'óltyy]	yellow
женщина	[ž'énš'ina]	woman
животное	[živótnoye]	animal

– З з –

завтра	[závtra]	tomorrow
завтрак	[závtrak]	breakfast
зелёный	[z'el'ónyy]	green

– И и –

июль	[iyúl']	July
июнь	[iyún']	June

– К к –

книга	[kníga]	book
корова	[koróva]	cow
кость	[kost']	bone
кофе	[kóf'e]	coffee
кошка	[kóška]	cat
красный	[krásnyy]	red
кровь	[krov']	blood

– Л л –

лёд	[l'od]	ice
лицо	[litsó]	face
лодка	[lódka]	boat
лошадь	[lóšad']	horse
луна	[luná]	moon

– М м –

магазин	[magazín]	store / shop
май	[mai]	May
маленький	[mál'en'kiy]	small
мальчик	[mál'čik]	boy
мама	[máma]	mommy / mama
март	[mart]	March
мать	[mat']	mother
машина	[mašína]	car (automobile)
месяц	[m'ésyats]	month
молоко	[molokó]	milk
море	[mór'e]	sea
Москва	[moskvá]	Moscow
мужчина	[mužčína]	man
мышь	[myš']	mouse
мясо	[m'áso]	meat

– Н н –

небо	[n'ébo]	sky
нет	[n'et]	no
нога	[nogá]	foot / leg
нос	[nos]	nose
ноябрь	[noyábr']	November

– О о –

обед	[ob'éd]	lunch
огонь	[ogón']	fire
одежда	[od'éžda]	clothing
один	[odín]	one
озеро	[óz'ero]	lake
окно	[oknó]	window
октябрь	[oktyábr']	October
отец	[ot'éts]	father

– П п –

папа	[pápa]	daddy / papa
парк	[park]	park
пиво	[pívo]	beer
платье	[plát'ye]	dress
плохой	[ploxóy]	bad
поезд	[póyezd]	train
понедельник	[pon'edél'nik]	Monday
птица	[ptítsa]	bird
пятница	[pyátnitsa]	Friday
пять	[pyat']	five

– P p –

ребёнок	[reb'ónok]	child
река	[r'eká]	river
ресторан	[restorán]	restaurant
Россия	[rosíya]	Russia
рот	[rot]	mouth
рубашка	[rubáška]	shirt
рука	[ruká]	hand / arm
русский	[rúskiy]	Russian
рыба	[rýba]	fish
рынок	[rýnok]	market

– C c –

самолёт	[samol'ót]	airplane
свинья	[svin'yá]	pig
сегодня	[s'evódnya]	today
семь	[s'em']	seven
сентябрь	[s'entyábr']	September
сердце	[s'érdts'e]	heart
сестра	[s'estrá]	sister
синий	[síniy]	blue
снег	[sn'eg]	snow
собака	[sobáka]	dog
солнце	[sólnts'e]	sun
среда	[sr'edá]	Wednesday
стол	[stol]	table
страна	[straná]	country (state)
стул	[stul]	chair
суббота	[subbóta]	Saturday
счастливый	[sčastlívyy]	happy

сын	[syn]	son
сыр	[syr]	cheese

– Т т –

тело	[t'élo]	body
три	[tri]	three
туфля	[túflya]	shoe

– У у –

ужин	[úžin]	dinner
улица	[úlitsa]	street
университет	[univ'ersit'ét]	university
ухо	[úkho]	ear

– Ф ф –

февраль	[f'evrál']	February

– Х х –

хлеб	[khl'eb]	bread
холодный	[kholódnyy]	cold
хороший	[khoróšiy]	good

– Ц ц –

цвет	[tsv'et]	color
цветок	[tsv'etók]	flower
церковь	[ts'érkov']	church

– Ч ч –

чай	[čai]	tea
час	[čas]	hour
человек	[č'elov'ék]	person
чёрный	[č'órnyy]	black
четверг	[č'etv'érg]	Thursday
четыре	[četýr'e]	four

– Ш ш –

шесть	[š'est']	six
школа	[škóla]	school
шляпа	[šl'ápa]	hat

– Я я –

| яблоко | [yábloko] | apple |
| январь | [yanvár'] | January |

Other language learning titles available from Wolfedale Press:

Learn to Read Arabic in 5 Days
Learn to Read Armenian in 5 Days
Learn to Read Bulgarian in 5 Days
Learn to Read Georgian in 5 Days
Learn to Read Greek in 5 Days
Learn to Read Modern Hebrew in 5 Days
Learn to Read Persian (Farsi) in 5 Days
Learn to Read Ukrainian in 5 Days

77503608R00031

Made in the USA
Middletown, DE
21 June 2018